"I want to remain kind despite my anger."

- Kuma

For all of us.

AUGUST

Published July 2023 by
DeepRichDirt Publishing LLC
Wagram, NC

www.DeepRichDirt.com

December

The morning after you died

The sun rose

Coffee was brewed

Feedthecatswalkthedogbrushmyteeth

I go through the motions

When there were three

There is now one

I feel the weight of women before me

I feel their hands

On my shoulders, on my chest, down my throat

Grabbing

Searching

Pleading

For me to understand

They stare back at me in the mirror

"You're a woman now"

They whisper

I want to scream

"I always have been."

January

Frost is settling over the valley now
Winter's cold kiss
Beckoning me below the waters
"drown"
A voice whispers
"I have to stay"
I whisper back
A certain numbness takes over
Snow crunches around my boots
Empty prescription bottles litter the sink
Orange never was my favorite color
Too bright
Harsh
I'd rather crawl into a dark hole
Than be reminded
I throw away the empty pill bottles
And allow myself to cry

February

I can't sit around crying for months

So, I go out with my friend

Paint my lips ruby red

Sip overpriced cocktails in some dimly lit bar

We talk shit about men, and the curse of now
having to consider Botox

Even though we're still in our twenties

We say our hazy goodbyes, drunk on laughs and
femininity

I get in my car

Close the door

And cry

Sobs, heavy and thorough, wrack my frame

I drive home numb, mascara streaming down my
face

Screaming into the darkness

Wishing

Hoping

Praying

That something or someone is listening

March

Sometimes, I feel it's easier to drown

Swimming takes energy; Strength

I don't have either

Is it a strength to admit when I'm too weak to help myself?

I lie in bed

Heart breaking wide open

Bleeding

Bleeding

Bleeding

I don't want to fight

I'm so tired of fighting my body

My *home*

The only true home a woman can have is her body

so

How could I hate myself,

When I was your home?

April

In my dreams
Your father and I hold you
You have his hair
Sunlight flickers through the trees
He makes us laugh, like always

This is all I've ever wanted.

At our next appointment
I ask the doctor for sleep medication
In hopes that
The dreams will stop

May

Winter breaks

Spring arrives slowly

The birds return from the south

Snow melts

Anger

Bright and bitter

Courses through every part of me; runs through
my veins

Anger or grief?

It's all the same

I find refuge in women

None of the male doctors seem to understand

It has been women

This entire time

Holding my hand

Guiding me through the dark

I whisper to the trees

"I understand now."

June

Flowers greet me

Bowing their heads under the heavy sun

I sit on front porches with wise women

They rock in their chairs and tell me secrets only
women know

I gasp at the light

There is so much life to live

On the other side of pain

Hello, hello, hello

I whisper

We are so glad you're still here

The evergreens whisper back

July

Healing comes slowly

Then

All at once

I am awakened

Women's laughter

Seeps into my pores, filling up every crevasse
that you left

It was women all along

My mother looks at me in a different way

Or maybe it's me finally understanding

The sacrifices women make

I tell only a few trusted people

And sometimes strangers

I make new, older, wiser friends

Women who are smart

And kind

And don't judge me for the choices I made

August

We silently watch as

Ashes rise on the wind

Scattering amongst the pines

The trees observe me in solemn silence

"You would have been an amazing mom"

He whispers

I smile

"I know."

A gentle summer's breeze brushes my cheek

Robins call to each other from across the glen

I feel my solid feet

Planted firmly in the deep, rich dirt

Reminding me of where we come from

And where we shall all

Return

FIN.

Acknowledgements

I couldn't have gotten this far without the support of many incredible women in my life. Over the course of this year, I have found it has been women, time and time again, who have caught me when I stumbled. Perfection does not exist. And I am forever grateful for the grace, patience, and everlasting kindness these women have shown me as I've grown. The following people have watched with non-judgement as I stumble, my heart on my sleeve, tender belly-up, into this wide, wide world of womanhood: Shauni, Piper, Olivia, Haley, Nina, Tay, Cleo, all the new friends I've made this year, and to all my friends from years past. Thank you for everything; I truly do love being a woman because you all have shown me how glorious it is to be one.

Here's to many more over-priced cocktails in dimly lit bars.

To my publishers, Nate and Amanda Crew: Thank you for believing in this project. This writing was a genre in which I never thought we would explore together, yet it came together so naturally. Your enduring support and unwavering faith are something I will never forget. This is just the beginning of our collaboration. I'm beyond excited to see what the future has in store for us all!

To my editor Jess: I know we technically didn't work together on this project, but I want to thank you for sticking with me this far in our careers. It is a simple joy to watch you grow and meet fellow authors you also work with. I cannot wait to share *City of Kings and Killers* with you!

Thank you to all the medical professionals who helped me during the course of writing this book. Healthcare is a human right, and no one should ever be denied access to care.

To my family: Somehow, despite all the trauma, we all came out okay. (*This is a joke; please don't bring this up at Thanksgiving*). I love you all so much. Your enduring support, warm and guiding, has helped me become the woman I am today.

And lastly, thank you, dear reader. I wouldn't be here without you. Your belief in me, courage to read this book, and time spent with my words, is something that I will always be grateful for. I hope that wherever you are, you choose to stand for what you believe in, even if you're standing alone.

Until next time.

-L. Holmes

More from L. Holmes

City of Flame and Ash

City of Kings and Killers
- Coming 2024

About the Author

L. Holmes is a classically, internationally trained actress. She speaks Russian and English. As well as pursuing a Doctorate in medicine, she is a Certified Medical Coder and Medical Assistant. She is the founder of the American Authors' Union, as well as "The Protagonist", a podcast.

In her free time, she and her husband enjoy hiking, yoga, and spending time with their many animals. *August* is her debut poetry book. *City of Flame and Ash* is her debut adult fantasy novel.

Made in the USA
Middletown, DE
14 October 2023

40519526R00017